THE KEY
TO HAPPINESS

By Sophia Bedford-Pierce

Illustrated by Jo Gershman

PETER PAUPER PRESS, INC.
WHITE PLAINS, NEW YORK

Designed by Arlene Greco

In memory of Grandpa Herman,
who asked for little, received less,
and shared whatever he had

Copyright © 1997
Peter Pauper Press, Inc.
202 Mamaroneck Avenue
White Plains, NY 10601
ISBN 0-88088-822-9
Printed in China
7 6 5 4 3 2 1

THE KEY
TO HAPPINESS

INTRODUCTION

Happiness means different things to different people. It is not, however, a face to be put on, or a pose. Happiness in its fullness is a state of being. There is neither a single key to happiness nor only one door. The rhythms and rhymes of life lead you to

the thresholds of many doors.
Choose the key that fits most
comfortably in your hand. Then
try it again and again until you
can unlock your own
happiness.

S. B.-P.

Happiness is life-affirming
and offers a sparkling glimpse
of the infinite.

The key dwells within you.

Do not confine your feelings of happiness to a time, a place, or an event—and your potential will flow without limit.

Saying "yes" does not insure happiness. Saying "no" does not necessarily turn it away. Finding the word that matches your conviction is the key.

The tributaries of the river of
experience are the streams of
new beginnings.

Y ou may derive pleasure from a special possession; happiness, however, is not inherent in the possession itself.

Finding happiness does not
require a miracle, but an
appreciation of the miraculous
often helps.

You cannot command someone to be happy. Sharing your joy, however, will enrich those with whom it is shared.

Happiness is a state, but it is also a stage. Change, grow, mature–and the layers of happiness will unfold.

The practice of happiness may
require effort. But as you
identify what nourishes you,
happiness comes with ever
less effort.

Too much time spent
searching for happiness leaves
too little time to recognize it.

Happiness is not measured by weight or distance but by the intensity of its light.

Be steady in your faith and your grasp on happiness will be firm.

When you can identify what
you need and choose what
you want, you can overcome
all obstacles.

The key to happiness will
unlock the door of your life.
Use it every day.

The essence of happiness is
constant; its form, however, is
subject to change.

The truest description of
yourself should be written in
your own hand.

The something that you may desire to be is of less value than the character of the someone you are.

The only way to practice living is to live. The only way to begin to do so is to begin.

Spend less time counting
your blessings and more time
sharing them.

Be clear about your own
nature. Know yourself well.
With clarity comes happiness.

At the end of this rainbow is
the other end of the rainbow,
but you are standing here now
and the colors of the spectrum
are no less radiant.

Embrace what you know to be
important.

Let yourself feel happiness
and you ennoble yourself in
the process.

You would go quickly to your
friends in their time of sorrow.
Go to them also in their time
of joy.

You can create or receive
happiness only if you have a
sense of well-being.

Even the sweetest song will
sound sour if you do not sing it
in your own key.

Walk to the beat of your own drummer and you can carry the tune of your heart's own melody.

The lessons learned at leisure prepare you to take the actions that sustain you in times of need.

Without self-knowledge
happiness is transient.

Caring is the act of a builder.
Carelessness undermines the
structure.

There are ways unnumbered
of welcoming happiness into
your life.

Practice forgiveness and you
clear the way for renewal
and growth.

If you are disrespectful of others, how must you see yourself?

Advice that is uninformed by
wisdom lies flat on the page
and is of little practical use.

advice
that
is
uninformed by
wisdom lies in
on the pac...

and is of little
PRACTICAL use

Do not try to reshape your friends. Treasure them because you can embrace the substance of who they are.

Acts of kindness are carried out
by a gentle hand; compassion is
more demanding; love at its
fullest is all-encompassing;
happiness is the thread that
runs like a lifeline through
them all.

The path to inner peace and happiness can be enriched by memories. It cannot, however, be memorized.

When you postpone the acceptance of love you steal time from the fullness of life.

When the dancer becomes
one with the dance, joy is
visible.

Teach by example and you will expend fewer words while accomplishing more.

An open and loving heart is
the passkey to life's most
meaningful riches.

A tear from laughter is liquid joy.

Enlightenment is the ultimate
manifestation of happiness.

No sunrise is greeted as warmly
as the one seen through
sparkling eyes.

Ignoring what others say is an exercise in choice. Ignoring your inner voice is a recipe for unhappiness.

Sadness wanes where happiness
is emergent.

Let your actions be your
signature and you will be
assured of having a
good name.

Things difficult to understand are made less so by asking questions. Refusing to ask questions postpones understanding indefinitely.

The making of an artist is within you. Find your own medium, or risk a house of empty canvases.

The key to security is in an
unlocked heart.

Spare no effort in laying a
foundation if you wish that
which you build to endure.

All the energy of the universal force has been brought to bear to create you–and a singular grain of sand.

Each season leaves its mark so that the new season knows where to start.

You cannot ask your guests
to have a happy stay if you
have not made provisions
for their comfort.

Ignorance fuels mistrust.
Mistrust insures misunderstanding. Misunderstanding
corrupts the language of hope,
and lays waste the promise of
happiness.

Although the truth may not be subject to interpretation, the language you choose to convey the facts requires sensitivity.

If opportunity knocks before
you have the key to the door,
ask it to come in through
the window.

Hold close that you which you
treasure, and you touch one life.
Share your treasure willingly
and you touch the lives of all
whom you meet.

If you seek glory for the glow,
glory will elude you or prove
hollow when held.

Strive for good health; seek lasting friendships; permit joy to enter your sphere; let your actions be governed by a sense of honor; and happiness will come unbidden.

What you judge to be authentic
will not disappoint you.

Do not regret the path not taken. See the road that you are on as the path to endless opportunities.

The key to happiness unlocks
the door of wonder.

Life's most vital forces thrive in
the presence of joy.